BUILDING SNOW FORTS

By Dana Meachen Rau • Illustrated by Kathleen Petelinsek

CHERRY LAKE PUBLISHING • ANN ARBOR, MICHIGAN

CHERRY LAKE Publishing

Published in the United States of America by Cherry Lake Publishing
Ann Arbor, Michigan
www.cherrylakepublishing.com

Content Adviser: Dr. Julia L. Hovanec, Department of Art Education and Crafts, Kutztown University of Pennsylvania, Kutztown, Pennsylvania

Photo Credits: Page 4, ©Monkey Business Images/Dreamstime.com; page 5, ©Martinmark/Dreamstime.com; page 6, ©Tetyana Kochneva/Dreamstime.com; page 7, ©Terric Delayn/Shutterstock, Inc.; page 8, ©Accent Alaska.com/Alamy; page 9, ©ASSOCIATED PRESS; pages 13 and 14, ©Tyler Olson/Shutterstock, Inc.; page 15, ©Suzanne Tucker/Shutterstock, Inc.; page 29, ©Agencyby/Dreamstime.com; page 32, ©Tania McNaboe

Library of Congress Cataloging-in-Publication Data
Rau, Dana Meachen, 1971–
Building snow forts / by Dana Meachen Rau.
p. cm. — (How-to library. Crafts)
Includes bibliographical references and index.
ISBN 978-1-61080-469-1 (lib. bdg.) —
ISBN 978-1-61080-556-8 (e-book) — ISBN 978-1-61080-643-5 (pbk.)
1. Snow forts—Juvenile literature. 2. Structural engineering—Juvenile literature. I. Title.
 TH1431.R38 2012
693'.91—dc23   2012009950

Cherry Lake Publishing would like to acknowledge the work of The Partnership for 21st Century Skills. Please visit www.21stcenturyskills.org for more information.

Printed in the United States of America
Corporate Graphics Inc.
July 2012
CLFA11

HOW-TO LIBRARY

TABLE OF CONTENTS

Fun in the Snow…4

Weather Watch…6

Constructing with Snow…8

Basic Tools…10

Building Up Snow…12

Carving Out Snow…14

Castle Fortress…16

Erupting Volcano…18

Stairs and Slide…20

Target Toss…22

Snow Sofa…24

Glowing Color Column…26

Waiting for Snow…29

Glossary…30

Decorate with Flags…30

For More Information…31

Index…32

About the Author…32

Fun in the Snow

Tossing snowballs is a lot of fun!

Snow day! Get out the sleds and tubes. Strap on some skis and snowshoes. Snow is fun for winter sports.

Snow is also the perfect material for other games. Stretch out on the ground and make a snow angel. Roll huge mounds of snow to create a snowman. Pack a bunch of snowballs to toss with your friends. It's fun to have a shelter to hide in, too. Building a snow fort is a creative way to spend a snowy day.

So zip up a warm jacket, pull on your boots, and put on some waterproof gloves or mittens. Then get outside and start building!

BUNDLE UP

Just because the sun is shining doesn't mean it's warm outside! Be sure to wear layers of clothing when you go outside to build a snow fort. Start with long underwear on the top and bottom. Next, slip on a shirt or two, and pants. Then add a waterproof layer, such as snow pants and a coat. Be sure to wear warm socks, boots, a hat, and mittens.

If the day is extremely cold, you have to be careful of the parts of you that are not covered by clothing. Cold temperatures can cause **frostbite** on your skin. Don't stay out too long. Take frequent breaks inside to warm up.

Have you ever tried making a snow angel?

Weather Watch

Everything looks different after a snowstorm.

Have you ever wondered what clouds are made of? Clouds contain **water vapor**. Water vapor is water in the form of a gas. Clouds also contain tiny bits of dust. Water droplets may form around these bits of dust. The droplets freeze if the cloud is cold enough. As more water vapor sticks to a frozen droplet and freezes, a snow **crystal** will start to form.

The six-sided crystal can grow in a variety of ways. Sometimes it looks like a **hexagon**. It may grow like a column. It sometimes grows arms and branches. As it grows, it gets heavy. It falls down through the clouds. Snow crystals clump together to form snowflakes.

TAKE A CLOSER LOOK

Take a close look at some snowflakes the next time it snows. Bring a magnifying glass outside. Let some snowflakes fall on the sleeve of your jacket. If your jacket is a dark color, they will be even easier to see. Look closely at the crystals. Try again on another snowy day. Do the crystals look the same every time?

Snow crystals form into a variety of beautiful shapes.

Constructing with Snow

Some people still build igloos today.

People have built some amazing structures out of ice. For hundreds of years, the Inuit people of the Arctic have built igloos to shelter themselves from the cold. They cut blocks out of the hard snow on the ground to build these dome-shaped structures. A tunnel entrance helps trap the cold air so that the inside of the igloo stays warm. A hole in the top of the igloo acts as a chimney.

Snow builders construct snow castles, forts, and sculptures at winter festivals in cold areas such as Canada and Finland. The Snow Castle of Kemi in Finland is built every year in December. Then it is open to the public from January to April. It has many rooms to tour. It even has a restaurant and hotel rooms. It is built completely of snow.

Thousands of people visit the Snow Castle of Kemi each year.

Basic Tools

There are two ways to build and sculpt snow forts and other structures. You can either build them up with snow or carve them out of snow. You'll need different tools for each technique.

To Build Up Snow
- *Snow shovels*—to help you dig, plow, and lift snow
- *Snow brick maker or plastic shoebox*—to mold small rectangular snow bricks
- *Plastic tote bins or recycling bins*—to mold large rectangular snow bricks
- *Plastic sand pails*—to mold small **cylinders** of snow
- *Plastic garbage pails*—to mold large cylinders of snow

To Carve Out Snow
- *Plastic mixing spoons*—to dig out small details
- *Plastic spatulas*—to smooth out surfaces

Gather your tools before you get started.

FIND A FRIEND!
You can make some snow structures by yourself. But it is easier with a friend. Bins full of snow can be heavy. Things will go faster with someone to help. Best of all building with a friend is a lot more fun!

To Decorate Snow

- *Spray bottles, water, and food coloring—* to spray on snow to give it color
- *Natural items, such as branches, pinecones, and rocks—* to add decorative details to your snow creations

Stores sell plastic snow brick makers and snowball makers to help you mold snow. But don't worry if you don't have these items. Any plastic bin or pail will work just as well to make bricks. Use your hands to make great snowballs.

Building Up Snow

You have all the tools you need. Your head is filled with great ideas. Now you just need some snow!

Molding Methods

You can use various molds to form snow into shapes. Scoop snow into smaller molds, such as snow brick makers or sand pails, with your hands. Use a snow shovel to fill larger molds, such as large tote bins or garbage cans. Pack the snow down into your mold with your hands or the back of the shovel. The more **compact** the snow, the more solid your bricks will be when you unmold them.

After a mold is filled to the top, it is ready to flip over. If possible, unmold it onto the space where you want it. If your brick is well packed, you may be able to unmold it and then move it to where you want it to go.

You'll need two people to flip and unmold larger bricks. Ask a friend or adult to help you, especially if you are lifting the brick onto a second higher layer.

Sometimes snow will stick to the inside of your mold. You can prevent this by spraying a thin layer of cooking spray on the inside of your mold before packing snow into it.

Making a Mound

Instead of building with bricks, you can also build up a mound of snow. Use a snow shovel to dig snow from the ground or off a driveway or walkway, and start piling it up. Pat down each load with the back of your shovel as you dump it onto the pile. This will help compact the snow. Climbing over the pile will help pack it down, too. You can even let your mound sit for a day or so before you work with it. The snow will settle and pack down even more.

Sometimes mounds are already made for you. You can build a structure out of a snowbank along the edge of a shoveled driveway. A windy blizzard may have blown large **snowdrifts** that you can make into structures, too.

You can turn a mound of snow into a fun hideout.

Carving Out Snow

Once you've made a mound or a structure of snow bricks, you can carve shapes into it. Use a snow shovel to carve out steps or ledges into a snowbank or mound. Smooth out the snow with a spatula or your hands. Then use a plastic mixing spoon to add details. You can scoop out chunks of snow with the spoon end or cut out smaller bits with the handle end.

You can also carve windows into a snow wall. Carefully dig a hole on one side of the wall. Start small and then widen

Tunnels let you get in and out of your fort.

Make sure your tunnels are big enough to crawl through.

your circle. Eventually you will break through the wall. Carve the hole wider from the other side. Smooth out the opening with your hands or a spatula.

You can make a tunnel through snow. Start digging from one side and then from the other until the two tunnels meet. Make sure the walls are at least a foot thick and don't ever dig a tunnel by yourself. If you were alone and the tunnel caved in, no one would be able to help you. Always make sure someone is outside the tunnel while you are in it. Never climb on top of a tunnel when someone is inside.

Castle Fortress

You can build a strong fort out of snow bricks.

Build a safe shelter for protection from the wind, snow, or flying snowballs!

Materials

Snow brick maker or plastic shoebox
Sand pail
Pinecones or pebbles

Steps

1. Find a flat area to make your fort. Draw lines in the snow with a stick to map out the **perimeter**. The fort should have four sides with an opening on one side for your door.

16

2. Pack your brick maker with snow and unmold the brick along your line. Continue making and placing bricks along the perimeter. Place them as close together as possible.

3. Next comes the second layer. Pack your brick maker and unmold it on top of the first layer of bricks. Don't line up the second layer of bricks with the ones directly below. The lines between the bricks should be **staggered**. This will make your wall stronger and more solid.

Don't line up each side of a brick with the sides of the brick below it.

4. Make a third layer and a fourth layer. Add even more layers if you want higher castle walls.

5. Next, add battlements to the walls. Pack a sand pail with snow. Unmold the snow on top of the wall. Repeat around the whole wall, leaving spaces in between.

6. Dig out windows in some of the walls, if you want to. (*See directions on pages 14–15.*) Add pinecones or pebbles around the doorway for a royal jeweled entrance fit for a king or queen.

Erupting Volcano

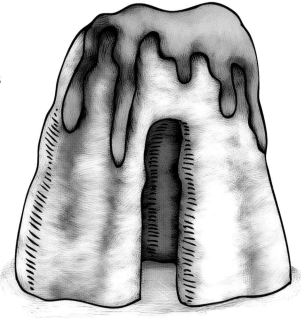

This cone-shaped fort looks like a volcano. Surprise your friends when it starts erupting with snowballs.

Materials

Snow shovel
Plastic garbage can
Large plastic rectangular
   tote bin
Lid of the tote bin
Large sand pail
Spray bottle, water, and yellow
   and red food coloring

Unlike real volcanoes, yours will be freezing cold!

Steps

1. Find a large, flat area to make your fort. Use a plastic garbage can to make eight large cylinders of snow. Place them in a circle shape. Leave an opening big enough for you to get into the circle. Fill in all of the other cracks between the cylinders with snow so that you have a solid base.

Stack smaller snow bricks on top of the large ones.

2. Use a large rectangular tote bin to mold the next layer. Make and place molded rectangles on top of the first layer. Fill in all the cracks with snow.

3. Place the lid of the tote across the top of your entrance. Cover it with snow. This will help support the third layer and create a doorway.

4. Use a large sand pail to build the third layer. Make and place the cylinders of snow on top of the second layer. Place them as close together as you can. You may need a step stool or a tall adult to help you if your structure is getting too high. Fill in all the cracks with snow.

5. Smooth out the sides of your volcano with a spatula or your hands.

6. Fill a spray bottle with water and add a few drops each of red and yellow food coloring. This will make an orange lava color! Spray it down the sides of your volcano so that it looks like lava dripping down the sides of a mountain.

7. Hide inside and toss snowballs out the top!

Stairs and Slide

Go for a ride on this speedy slide!

You'll need a pile of snow for this project. You may already have a big mound along the side of a driveway to get you started. If not, find an open area to build your snowy playground.

Materials

Snow shovel
Plastic sled or snow tube

Steps

1. Make a mound of snow about as high as your chest. As you add shovelfuls of snow, pack them down with the back of the shovel.

Carve your mound into the correct shape.

2. Start carving out steps. Dig into the edge of the mound and scoop out a shovelful of snow. Scoop at a slight angle downward into the mound. Use your hands or the shovel to pack the step down well.

3. Dig a second step above the first one.

4. Continue making and packing steps until you reach the top of your mound.

5. Stand at the base of the slide side. Use the back of the shovel to scrape snow from the high point at the top of your steps toward the base of the slide.

6. Climb the steps back to the top and scrape snow off the slide from that end, too. Continue to shape the slide to get the angle you want. Add more snow to the bottom to extend your slide, if you want to.

7. Ride a plastic sled or snow tube down your slide to smooth it out. Do this a few times to flatten any rough snow and help pack it down so that you can ride down it smoothly without the sled or tube.

Target Toss

Create a game to play with friends.

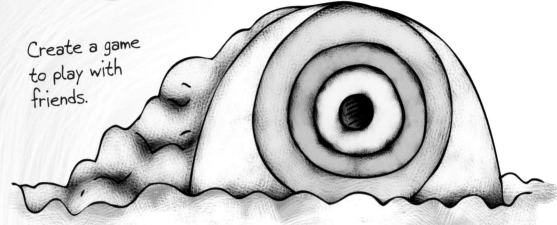

Invite a bunch of friends over to make a large batch of snowballs. Then compete to see who can score the most points in this winter twist on archery.

Materials

Plastic spatula
Plastic mixing spoon
3 spray bottles
Water
3 colors of food coloring

Steps

1. Find a snowbank or a snowdrift, or make a mound of snow. Use the spatula to flatten and smooth out one side of the mound so you have a large flat area that you can use as a target.

Dig your hole in the center of the mound.

2. In the center, dig out a deep hole with the plastic spoon. Make it as deep as your arm can reach in. Make it a little wider than the width of your arm.

3. Use the handle end of the spoon to draw a circle about 12 inches from the center hole. Draw another circle about 12 inches (30 centimeters) from the first one. Draw a third circle 12 inches from the second one. Adjust the size of your circles as needed, depending on the size of your mound.

4. Fill the spray bottles with water and add different colors of food coloring to each. Spray the first color inside the first circle. Fill in the second circle with the second color and the third circle with the last color.

5. Decide how many points each circle will be worth. Perhaps the outer circle can be 5 points, the middle circle 10, the inner circle 20, and the hole 50.

6. Stand about 10 yards (9 meters) away from your target. Throw snowballs at the target. Give your friends a turn. Keep score to see who wins.

Snow Sofa

It's time to take a seat!

All of this hard work building with snow may tire you out. You need a place to sit down! Make yourself a sofa of snow to take a well-deserved break.

Equipment

Large plastic tote bin
Plastic spatula
Plastic mixing spoon

Steps

1. Find a flat area for your snow sofa. Fill the large tote bin with snow and pack it well. Flip it over and unmold it. Make and place another large brick next to it. Then make and place two more bricks behind them. Now you have a large rectangle of bricks.

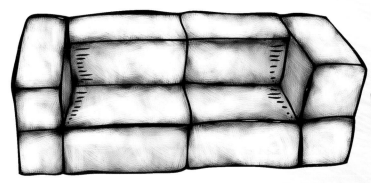

Make sure your bricks are packed well.

2. Make and place a brick on each end of the rectangle.
3. Build a second layer of bricks on top of the two bricks in the back of the rectangle.
4. Build a second layer on top of the two bricks on each end of the rectangle.
5. Fill in all of the cracks and gaps with snow. Then smooth out the surfaces with a spatula or with your hands.
6. Use a plastic spoon to carve details onto your sofa. Round out the armrests on each side. Carve cushion shapes in the back and the seat. Add wiggly lines of snow fringe along the bottom. Build a snow cat asleep in the corner. Then sit down and relax!

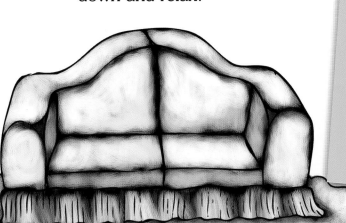

SNOW FURNITURE
You can make all kinds of furniture out of snow. Make snow chairs around a snow table. Then set it up with an outdoor snack. Or make a snow bed to take a rest in the open air.

Glowing Color Column

This colorful column can light your yard at night.

You'll need a few days of freezing temperatures for this snow structure. Blocks of colored ice and a hidden flashlight will make this tower glow.

Materials

13 empty and clean half-gallon (2 liter)
    orange juice or milk cartons
Water
Food coloring in various colors
Scissors
Branches from pine trees
String
Flashlight

RECYCLING!
You may not have 13 empty orange juice or milk cartons on hand for this project. Save them up so that you have them when you need them. You can also ask friends and neighbors to save some for you.

Don't fill your cartons too high. Stop where the sides start to slant.

Steps

1. Fill 12 of the cartons with water to the top of the rectangular part of the carton. Add a few drops of food coloring. Hold the tops of the cartons closed and gently shake the cartons to mix up the color. You can also mix different food colorings to create new colors!

2. Place the cartons upright in a shaded area outside. Leave them to freeze overnight or until the water turns into solid bricks of ice.

3. Prepare your last carton to be a snow brick maker. Cut off the spout end and then cut off one of the sides. Now you have a brick maker the same size and shape as your ice bricks.

4. Unwrap your ice bricks by ripping apart the cartons. You should have 12 colorful bricks.

5. Find a good location for your tower. Use your brick maker to make four packed, solid snow bricks. Place the snow bricks in a square shape so there is a hole in the center.

6. For the next layer, place four ice bricks on top of the snow bricks. Stagger them so that the lines between the top bricks aren't lined up with the ones below.

Stack your bricks as neatly as possible.

7. For the third layer, make and place four more snow bricks. Again, make sure you stagger the lines between the brick layers.

8. Continue **alternating** between layers of ice bricks and snow bricks. End with a snow layer.

9. Collect pine branches from the yard. Lay them on top of your column like a roof. Tie a string onto your flashlight and attach it to one of the branches so that it hangs down into the center of your tower.

10. When it gets dark outside, turn on the flashlight and watch your tower glow.

The flashlight will make your whole column light u

ICY WINDOWS
Ice bricks can also be used as windows in a fort such as the castle fortress on pages 16–17. You can add food coloring to your bricks or keep them clear.

Waiting for Snow

Some winters have record snowfalls. You may have so much snow that you can spend many days outside creating **elaborate** forts and other snow sculptures. During other winters, you may not see much snow at all. You may be waiting and waiting at the window, wishing the flakes would start to fall. And when it does snow, there's no guarantee that it will be the best packable kind to build a snow fort.

Use the time waiting for snow to make your own type of storm—a brainstorm! A brainstorm is a list of ideas. Get together some friends and write or draw all of your ideas. Ask yourselves questions. What would make an amazing fort? How high can you build it? What supplies will you need? What details and decorations can you add? Be sure to think big.

When the snow finally falls, you'll be ready to start building an amazing snow structure.

You can think up new ideas for snow forts no matter what the weather is like!

Glossary

alternating (AWL-tur-nay-ting) going back and forth between two things

compact (KAHM-pakt) packed in tightly

crystal (KRIS-tuhl) a substance that forms a pattern of flat surfaces when it is solid

cylinders (SIL-uhn-durz) three-dimensional shapes with two circular ends

elaborate (i-LAB-ur-it) complex and detailed

frostbite (FRAWST-bite) injury to the skin caused by extreme cold

hexagon (HEK-suh-gahn) a shape with six straight sides

perimeter (puh-RIM-i-tur) the outer boundary of a shape

snowdrifts (SNO-drifts) piles of snow formed by wind

staggered (STAG-urd) arranged in a way so that the objects don't line up

water vapor (WAW-tur VAY-pur) the gaseous form of water

Decorate with Flags

Decorate the corners of your castle fort or any snow structure with flags. Tie bandanas on the ends of sticks. Place them in the snow. If you don't have any bandanas, use paper or other fabric to design flags of your own!

For More Information

Books

Cassino, Mark. *The Story of Snow: The Science of Winter's Wonder.* San Francisco: Chronicle Books, 2009.

Libbrecht, Kenneth. *The Secret Life of a Snowflake: An Up-Close Look at the Art and Science of Snowflakes.* Minneapolis: Voyageur Press, 2009.

Ralston, Birgitta. *Snow Play: How to Make Forts & Slides & Winter Campfires, Plus the Coolest Loch Ness Monster and 23 Other Brrrilliant Projects in the Snow.* New York: Artisan, 2010.

Web Sites

KidsHealth: How to Be Safe in Ice and Snow

http://kidshealth.org/kid/watch/out/winter_safety.html

Find out why it's so important to dress warmly when you play in the snow.

Lumi Linna Snow Castle

www.snowcastle.net/en/homepage

Check out one of the world's most amazing snow forts.

SnowCrystals.com

www.its.caltech.edu/~atomic/snowcrystals

Learn more about the shapes of snow crystals and how they are formed.

Index

brainstorming, 29
building up, 10, 12–13

carving out, 10, 14–15
castle fortress project,
    16–17
clothing, 5
clouds, 6

decorations, 11
details, 10, 11, 14

erupting volcano project,
    18–19

festivals, 9
Finland, 9

frostbite, 5

glowing color column
    project, 26–28

igloos, 8
Inuit people, 8

molds, 10, 11, 12
mounds, 13, 14, 20

packing, 9, 12, 13, 29

recycling, 26

safety, 5, 15
snowballs, 9, 11, 22

Snow Castle of Kemi, 9
snow crystals, 6–7
snowdrifts, 13
snowflakes, 7
snow sofa project, 24–25
stairs and slide project,
    20–21

target toss project, 22–23
teamwork, 11, 12
temperatures, 5, 8, 26
tools, 10, 11, 12, 13, 14,
    15, 26
tunnels, 8, 15

water vapor, 6
windows, 14–15, 28

About the Author

Dana Meachen Rau is the author of more than 300 books for children on many topics, including science, history, cooking, and crafts. She creates, experiments, researches, and writes from her home office in Burlington, Connecticut.